THE CREED OF A
PRIEST OF SAVOY

JEAN-JACQUES ROUSSEAU

THE CREED OF A PRIEST OF SAVOY

Translated, with an introduction, by
ARTHUR H. BEATTIE
University of Arizona

FREDERICK UNGAR PUBLISHING CO.
NEW YORK

MILESTONES
OF THOUGHT
in the History of Ideas

Edited by
F. W. STROTHMANN
Stanford University

Copyright 1956 by
Frederick Ungar Publishing Co.

Printed in the United States of America

Library of Congress Catalog Card Number: 56-7501

INTRODUCTION

Eighteenth-century thought gives an important place to the related ideas of natural religion and of natural law. Even Christian theologians of that day would discuss at length the principles of natural religion as one element in their theology before turning to the specifically Christian doctrines of their revealed religion. Natural religion, or deism, includes those notions of God, the organization of the universe, man's relation to it, and his resultant obligations which the human reason, unaided by divine revelation, can presumably arrive at by logical processes. The deist differs from the atheist in his recognition of the existence of a divine Providence guiding the universe; if he remains merely a deist, if he does not utilize the principles of natural religion to bolster other beliefs accepted on faith, he differs from the Christian in his rejection of the element of the miraculous and of all doctrines which have their source in revelation.

By and large, the eighteenth-century thinker accepts the notion that this is a rational universe governed by law, and he therefore believes that to follow nature is to follow reason. It is the romantics of a later generation who substitute the notion that to follow nature is to follow passion and to free oneself from all laws and obligations. Like the Stoics of antiquity, the deist believes that there are principles of natural law which prevail for all men of all races, in all climates, and in all times. The laws of human societies are good in the degree that they approach the principles of that universal natural law which any man, unless thoroughly perverted, can find within his heart.

These notions of natural religion and natural law

ought not to be remote questions of purely academic interest to Americans of the twentieth century, for they are incorporated in the great documents of the American Revolution and, to some extent, in the institutions of our government. Tom Paine, Benjamin Franklin, Thomas Jefferson, and George Washington belong to the tradition of eighteenth-century deism. The opening sentence of the Declaration of Independence invokes the laws of nature and nature's God, and the very concept of unalienable rights is a recognition of universal law applicable to all mankind. Philosophically, the principles of the American Revolution stem from eighteenth-century rationalism. The close ties of Franklin and Jefferson with France serve to emphasize the important rôle of French thought in providing the intellectual background of American independence and nationhood.

Of the documents in which the doctrines of deism are expressed, few were so acclaimed in their day, and so bitterly assailed, as "The Creed of a Priest of Savoy," incorporated by Jean-Jacques Rousseau in his novel *Emile*, first published in 1762. Rousseau believed that this sincere expression of belief in God, in the human soul, and in principles of conduct derived from a concept of natural law, would win the favor of philosophers because it did not go beyond the limits of what the rationalist might accept, and would appease the Christians since it was not in conflict with their dogma and offered, indeed, a reasonable basis for a considerable portion of it. The attacks on this creed were immediate and violent. Some came from the *philosophes* who had some fifteen years earlier welcomed Rousseau, a newcomer from Switzerland, as a member of their band. Rousseau had not been restrained in his quarrels with Voltaire and others of this group. His profession of faith includes a denunciation of the doctrines of Diderot and of others of the atheist wing of the movement. But violent as were the attacks from his erstwhile friends, those of organized religions were bitterer still and far more dangerous. In Paris, Roman Catholic influence led to the burning of *Emile* and the issuance of a warrant for the arrest of the author. Friends helped him flee to Protestant Geneva, but the city of Calvin was no more tolerant than the French capital, and again Rousseau was obliged to seek safety in flight.

The popularity and influence of Rousseau's exposition of deism were nevertheless immense. One can scarcely exaggerate the enthusiasm with which his religious and moral teachings were received by thousands of disciples all over Europe. Letters sent to Rousseau by admirers reflect the ardor of persons of all classes, and of all professions and trades, whose lives had been illumined and altered by the fervor of his religious and moral teachings. He stirred the little shopkeeper and the semi-literate artisan, but the intellectual came under his spell too. Immanuel Kant could declare that no book had moved him so profoundly as *Emile*, and in the next generation Goethe could write that it is the gospel of all teachers.

Deism varies greatly from writer to writer. Unlike an organized religion, it has no set dogma. The deists are in accord with one another in recognizing the existence of a divine Providence, but their conclusions, based on the reason of the individual and not on authority, may differ widely on other points. Some, for example, declare the soul to be mortal, others immortal. The deism of Rousseau has its own accent. The age of reason was at the same time an age of sentiment, with a fondness for moralizing in the manner of Richardson and a marked propensity for shedding torrents of tears. Rousseau is, however, among the most sentimental men of his sentimental age, and his greater confidence in feeling than in reason makes his deism quite different in tone from the cold and intellectual deism of, for example, Voltaire. He is definitely of his age, yet his strong emphasis on sentiment makes of him a significant precursor of Romanticism.

Though Rousseau is distinguished from many of his

fellow philosophers of France by the more pronounced sentimental accent of his work, his criticisms of the British empiricists are made in the name of common sense. Common sense persuades him that the material universe does indeed exist, without reference to his perception of it. He cannot accept the notion that there are no innate ideas and that man is solely the product of his experiences. He cites the activities of his puppy to illustrate that instinct does exist in animals, and he remains convinced that somewhat analogous tendencies and powers are innate in man. Philosophically, Rousseau stands as a link between the empiricists and Kant.

Rousseau borrows his ideas from many sources, but any thinker must necessarily do so. Originality in thought doubtless consists more in the combining of ideas than in formulating ideas which no one has ever conceived before. It would be idle here to seek the sources of Rousseau's ideas. It must suffice for our purposes to note that he gives expression to ideas that are current in his generation, marking them distinctly at the same time with the imprint of a personality and a temperament which are his own.

Rousseau does not always construct his expositions with that inevitable logic which is frequently characteristic of French thought. The flow of his feelings, rather than the logic of a rigorously conceived plan, often determines the structure of the argument. "The Creed of a Priest of Savoy" is something of an exception to this principle. It is one of the best constructed of his writings. One may find in it repetitions, flaws in logic, and developments which seem trivial in our day, but the fact remains that it was in the eighteenth century a vital work whose impact on the thought of Europe was tremendous. It stands as one of the most thorough presentations of the concept of natural religion, and is therefore a document of capital importance in the history of ideas.

Its interest ought not to be purely historical, however. Recent scientific developments only emphasize the need for considering man's relationship to the universe and the moral bases for his relations with his fellow men. The problems which concern Rousseau are not without pertinence for today.

It is not possible here to recount in detail the life of Rousseau. A few biographical facts may however be noted briefly. He was born in 1712 in Geneva, son of an impractical watchmaker, afflicted with *Wanderlust*. His mother died shortly after giving birth to her son. Perhaps one may properly seek in the circumstances of his motherless childhood the origin of the mental disorders to which Jean-Jacques was later to be a prey. In any event, his upbringing was of the most unconventional sort. He learned to read during long vigils with his father in the course of which the child and the parent eagerly devoured long novels of romantic love. As a ragamuffin in the streets of Geneva, and as an apprentice to an engraver, the youngster added to his highly irregular education.

At the age of sixteen, Rousseau left Geneva, was converted to Catholicism, and came under the influence of Mme de Warens. This woman, who was eventually to be both mother and mistress to her young protégé, brought in time a measure of order into his life and gave him the opportunity to read abundantly and to acquire the education he had failed to receive through formal schooling. At the age of thirty, having served in capacities as varied as valet and music teacher, he arrived in Paris a well-read man bringing with him a new system of musical notation which helped him gain a certain reputation but no material success.

The important writings of Rousseau begin with his *Discourse on the Sciences and the Arts* of 1750, a prize-winning essay in a competition sponsored by the provincial Academy of Dijon. The ideas of Rousseau's apparently paradoxical thesis that the progress of the sciences and arts has been damaging to man's well-being were obviously in the air, otherwise the subject would not have been proposed for the competition. In any event, Rousseau is henceforth committed to the doctrine that the simple life close to nature is the best one, and that civilization is in reality a corrupting force. The second discourse, *On the Origin of Inequality*, of 1755, is a more dangerous one, for it deals with the question of private property as the cornerstone of an iniquitous social order which has perverted the fundamental natural goodness of man.

Rousseau withdrew from the artificial life of Parisian society, and sought to live according to the principles he had set forth in his discourses. From a semi-rustic retreat, he wrote *La Nouvelle Héloïse,* a novel which records his dreams of love and his sentimental concept of virtue. The book, which appeared in 1761, is one of the most widely read of its century. Before 1800 it had appeared in about seventy editions. And it was not read merely as a sentimental novel—its fervent readers took Rousseau as an inspired guide in matters of morals. In the meantime, this moralizing guide to virtue continued to live with his common-law wife whom he was not to marry legally until after she had borne him five children, each of whom in turn was abandoned at the door of the foundling hospital.

The year 1762 saw the publication of both *The Social Contract,* so influential upon the political thinking of the revolutionary era, and *Emile,* a novel which is at the same time a treatise on education. The young hero receives no religious instruction until he is fifteen, old enough to judge for himself the ideas which he adopts. Rousseau is eager that the child not have the beliefs of his family or his teachers inculcated in him at an age when he might uncritically accept them. "The Creed of a Priest of Savoy," an idealization of the guidance in religious thought which Rousseau himself had received from two priests when as a youth he fled from Geneva to Turin, is introduced to demonstrate the sort of instruction in religion which might be incorporated in the ideal program of education.

The years between the publication of *Emile* and the

death of Rousseau in 1778 were troubled ones, filled with persecutions, quarrels, disputes. Rousseau had long been ill physically, and he suffered, certainly, from a persecution mania. He had good reason to fear persecution, for he had genuinely been the victim of it. It is small wonder if at length he began to suspect his friends, those even who tried most sincerely to help him.

It is difficult to judge Rousseau, and difficult to refrain from judging him. It is best to look upon him as a man of undoubted genius who gave expression in moving and eloquent terms to an important segment of the thought of his age, and who exercised an influence beyond measure on the politics, literature, and thought of Europe.

A. B.

SELECTED BIBLIOGRAPHY

I. WORKS OF ROUSSEAU

1) The complete text of *Emile* is available in English as no. 518 in the Everyman Series, in a translation by Barbara Foxley, E.P. Dutton and Company, New York, 1911.
2) Selections from Rousseau, with an introduction by Romain Rolland, are to be found in *Rousseau*, in The Living Thoughts Library, David McKay and Co., Philadelphia, 1939.

II. WORKS ABOUT ROUSSEAU

1) Cassirer, Ernst, *The Question of Jean-Jacques Rousseau*, translated and edited by Peter Gay, Columbia University Press, New York, 1954.
2) Cresson, André, *Jean-Jacques Rousseau: sa vie son oeuvre, avec un exposé de sa philosophie*, Alcan, Paris, 1940.
3) Hendel, Charles William, *Jean-Jacques Rousseau, Moralist*, Oxford University Press, New York, 1934.
4) Lemaître, Jules, *Jean-Jacques Rousseau*, translated by Jeanne Mairet, William Heineman, London, 1908.
5) Masson, Pierre-Maurice, *La Formation religieuse de Jean-Jacques Rousseau*; *La Profession de Foi de Jean-Jacques*; *Jean-Jacques Rousseau et la restauration religieuse*; 3 vols., Hachette, Paris, 1916.
6) Morley, John, *Rousseau*, Macmillan and Co., New York, 1905.
7) Mornet, Daniel, *Rousseau, l'homme et l'oeuvre*, Boivin, Paris, 1950.
8) Schinz, Albert, *La Pensée religieuse de Rousseau et ses récents interprètes*, Alcan, Paris, 1927.

THE CREED OF A PRIEST OF SAVOY

Simple statement of belief of a peasant-born priest

My child, do not expect of me either learned speeches or profound reasoning. I am not a great philosopher, and I care little about being one. But I sometimes have good sense, and I always love truth. I don't want to argue with you, nor even to seek to convince you; it is enough for me if I set forth what I think in the simplicity of my heart. Consult your own heart as I speak; that is all I ask of you. If I am mistaken, it is in good faith; that is sufficient so that my error should not be held against me as a crime. Should you be mistaken similarly, there would be little harm in that. Since we are both reasonable creatures, and since we have the same interest in heeding reason, why should you not think as I do if I am right?

I was born a poor peasant, destined by my station in life to till the soil; but it was deemed preferable that I should learn to earn my living in the profession of a priest, and a way was found to send me to school. Certainly neither my parents nor myself thought much of seeking through my training what was good, true, or useful, but we were concerned with what I must know in order to be ordained. I learned what I was expected to learn, I said what I was expected to say, I took the vows that were expected of me, and I became a priest. But I wasn't long in realizing that in undertaking (by the vow of chastity) not to be a man, I had made promises beyond my power to keep.

Conscience follows law of nature

We are told that conscience is the product of prejudices; yet I know by

1

my own experience that it persists in following the order of nature against all the laws of man. Even though we may be forbidden to do this or that, we can never feel a strong remorse for doing what well-ordered nature permits us; above all, we cannot feel remorse for doing what nature commands. O good young man, nature has not yet spoken to your senses: live long in the happy state in which her voice is the voice of innocence. Remember that one offends her even more by yielding too quickly to her call than by struggling against it; one must begin by learning to resist in order to know when one may yield without crime.

Youthful   disgrace   of   the   priest   From my youth, I have respected marriage as the first and most sacred institution of nature. Having taken from myself the right to accept it, I resolved not to profane it; for, having always led a quiet and simple life, I had kept in my mind, in spite of my classes and my studies, the full force of the inborn light of conscience: the maxims of the world had not obscured it, and my poverty kept me away from those temptations which dictate the sophisms of vice.

This resolve was precisely what caused my ruin; my respect for the bed of others made my sins evident. The scandal had to be expiated; arrested, placed under an interdict, driven out, I was indeed more the victim of my scruples than of my incontinence; and I had reason to realize, by the reproaches which accompanied my disgrace, that often one has only to make the crime greater in order to escape punishment.

Attitude of uncertainty and doubt   It takes but few experiences of this sort to lead a reflective spirit far. By sad observations, seeing how the ideas I had of justice, honesty, and all the duties of man were overturned, I lost each day some one of the beliefs which I had heretofore accepted; those which remained being no longer sufficient to form a consistent set of principles, I felt little by little

2

the foundation of my belief grow weaker in my mind. Brought at length to the point where I didn't know what to think, I was in the same situation as yourself—with this difference, that my unbelief, late fruit of a more mature age, had been formed with more difficulty and was to be more difficult to destroy.

I was in that attitude of uncertainty and doubt which Descartes declares necessary for the pursuit of truth. That state is not one which can long endure, for it is disturbing and painful; only the habit of vice or slothfulness of soul can leave us in it. My heart was not sufficiently corrupt for me to find pleasure in that state; and nothing encourages more the habit of reflection than seeking satisfaction within oneself rather than in one's fortune.

I kept meditating, then, upon the sorry fate of mortals, adrift on this sea of human opinions, without a rudder, without a compass, and given over to their stormy passions, and without any other guide than an inexperienced pilot who fails to recognize his route and who knows not whence he comes nor where he goes. I kept saying to myself: "I love truth, I seek it, I cannot recognize it; let it be revealed to me, and I will remain firm in my acceptance of it. Why must it elude the eagerness of a heart made to worship it?"

Although I have often experienced greater woes, I have never led a life so constantly unpleasant as in those times of troubles and anxieties when, unceasingly wandering from doubt to doubt, I derived from my long meditations only uncertainty, obscurity, contradictions on the cause of my being and the law of my duties.

Sincere systematic skepticism not possible

How can one be a skeptic systematically and in good faith? I cannot understand it. Such philosophers either do not exist, or are the most unfortunate of men. Doubt about the things which it is important for us to know is a state too violent for the human mind: it cannot bear up under it for long.

3

The mind comes to a decision in spite of itself in one way or another, and it prefers to be mistaken rather than to believe in nothing.

Rejection of church doctrines and philosophical systems What increased my distress was that, having been born in a church which decides everything, which permits no doubt, the rejection of a single belief made me reject all the rest, and the impossibility of admitting so many absurd teachings turned me also against those others which were reasonable. By telling me, "Believe everything," they prevented me from believing anything, and I no longer knew what to accept.

I consulted the philosophers, I thumbed their books, I examined their various opinions. I found them all proud, assertive, dogmatic, even in their so-called skepticism, not recognizing their ignorance on any subject, proving nothing, mocking one another; and this mutual contempt, common to all, seemed to me the only point on which all are right. Triumphant when they attack, they are without vigor in defending themselves. If you weigh their arguments, you find they have valid ones only when they seek to destroy; if you take a poll, each is reduced only to his own vote; they are in agreement only to dispute—to listen to them was not the way to escape from my uncertainty.

We are ignorant, but vanity makes us defend our opinions I concluded that the inadequacy of the human mind is the first cause of that prodigious diversity of opinions, and that pride is the second. We cannot measure the immense creation, we cannot calculate the relationships between its parts; we do not know its first laws nor its final cause; we do not know ourselves; we know neither our nature nor our active principle; scarcely do we know whether man is a simple or a compound being; impenetrable mysteries surround us on all sides; they are outside the domain of our senses;

to pierce them we think we have intelligence, and we have only imagination. Each clears for himself, through this imaginary world, a path which he believes the right one; none can know whether his leads to the goal. Yet we wish to penetrate everything, to know everything. The only thing which we cannot do is to recognize our ignorance concerning what we cannot possibly know. We prefer to come to a conclusion at random, and to believe what is not, rather than confess that none of us can see what is. We are but a tiny part of a great whole whose limits are beyond our conceiving, and which is given over by its creator to our foolish disputes; we are vain enough to want to decide what this whole is in itself, and what we are in relation to it.

Even if philosophers were in a position to discover truth, who among them would be interested in it? Each knows well that his system is not better founded than the others; but he supports it because it is his. There is not a single one who, succeeding in recognizing the true and the false, would not prefer the falsehood which he has found to the truth discovered by another. Where is the philosopher who, for his own glory, would not readily deceive mankind? Where is he who, in the secret of his heart, sets for himself any other goal than to achieve distinction? If only he rise above the mass, if only he outshine the brilliance of his rivals, what more does he ask for? The essential thing is not to think as others do. Among believers, he is an atheist; among atheists, he would be a believer.

Accept ignorance, except where knowledge is vital

The first fruit which I drew from these reflections was to learn to limit my seeking to what interested me immediately, to be content with a profound ignorance about all the rest, and to worry myself, to the point of doubt, only about things which it was important for me to know.

5

Intuition the best guide I realized also that, far from ridding me of my useless doubts, philosophers would only multiply those which tormented me, and would resolve none of them. I took, then, another guide, and I said to myself: Let us consult the inner light; it will lead me astray less than philosophers lead me astray; or at least my error will be my own, and I shall be less corrupted following my own illusions than by giving myself over to their falsehoods.

Deism the most satisfying system Then, reviewing in my mind the various opinions which had one after another won me over since my birth, I saw that, although none of them was sufficiently self-evident to convince me immediately, they had varying degrees of plausibility, and that one gave or refused one's inner assent to them in different degrees. After this first observation, comparing one with another all these different ideas, without letting prejudices intervene, I found that the first and most common system was also the simplest and most reasonable, and that it lacked, to win the support of all, only the novelty of being the latest one proposed. Suppose that all your ancient and modern philosophers had first drawn all they could from their strange systems of forces, chance, fatalism, necessity, atoms, animate world, living matter, materialism of every sort; then suppose that after them all Clarke* came enlightening the world, announcing finally the Being of beings and the bestower of all good things. With what universal admiration, with what unanimous applause would men not have hailed this new system! How great they would have found it, how consoling, how sublime, how fit to elevate the soul, to provide a foundation for virtue, and at the same time how striking, how luminous, how simple, offering fewer incomprehensible

*Samuel Clarke, 1675-1729, theologian of the Church of England. His influential writings on natural religion include *Being and Attributes of God*, 1704, and *Evidences of Natural and Revealed Religion*, 1705. [Translator's note]

elements than there are absurd ones in any other system! I said to myself: Irresolvable objections are common to all systems, because man's mind is too limited to deal with them; these difficulties, then, do not invalidate one system more than another. But what a difference when one considers the direct proofs! That system alone which explains everything is to be preferred, is it not, when it offers no more difficulty than others?

Basic truths felt intuitively Bearing then within myself the love of truth as my sole philosophy, and as my sole method an easy and simple rule which frees me from the vain subtlety of arguments, I take up again, following this rule, the examination of the knowledge which interests me, resolved to accept as self-evident any knowledge to which, in the sincerity of my heart, I shall not be able to refuse my consent, to accept as true any knowledge which will appear to follow necessarily from the first, and to leave all other knowledge in doubt, without rejecting nor admitting it, and without tormenting myself about determining its validity when it leads to nothing useful in practice.

Self-examination: recognition of the self and the exterior world But who am I? What right have I to judge things? And what is it which determines my judgments? If they are a necessary consequence of the impressions which I receive, I weary myself in vain pursuing these questions; they will not be answered, or they will be answered by themselves without my striving to solve the problem. I must first, then, turn my eyes upon myself in order to know the instrument which I wish to use, and to know how far I can trust its use.

I exist, and I have senses by which I am affected. That is the first truth which strikes me, and to which I am forced to acquiesce. Have I a separate feeling of my own existence, or do I feel it only through my sensations? That is my first doubt, which is for the present impossible

7

for me to resolve: for being continually affected by sensations, either immediately, or through memory, how can I know whether the notion of my self is something apart from these same sensations, and if it can be independent of them?

My sensations take place within me, since they make me aware of my existence; but their cause is outside me, since they affect me in spite of myself, and it is not within my power to produce or exclude them. I conceive then clearly that my sensation which is within me, and its cause which is outside me, are not the same thing.

Thus, not only do I exist, but there exist other beings, namely the objects of my sensations; and even though these objects should be only ideas, still it is true that those ideas are not myself.

Now, everything which I feel outside myself and which acts on my senses, I call matter; and all the portions of matter which I conceive brought together to form individual beings, I call bodies. Thus all the disputes of the idealists and the materialists have no significance for me; their distinctions about the appearance and reality of bodies are idle fancies.

Faculty of judgment, of comparison Here I am, then, just as sure of the existence of the universe as of my own. Then I reflect upon the objects of my sensations; and finding within myself the faculty of comparing them, I feel myself endowed with an active force which previously I didn't know I had.

To perceive is to feel; to compare is to judge; judging and feeling are not the same thing. Through sensation, objects present themselves to me as separate, isolated entities, such as they are in nature; by comparison, I move them about, I transport them, so to speak, I superimpose one upon another to determine their difference or their similarity, and generally all their relationships. In my opinion, the distinctive faculty of the active or intelligent being is to be able to give a meaning to the word *is*. I seek in vain in the purely sensitive being this intelligent force which brings objects together and draws conclusions concerning them; I cannot see that power in its nature. That passive being will perceive each object separately, or even it will perceive the total object which two objects together form; but having no power to fit one to the other, it will never compare them, it will not judge them.

To see two objects at the same time is not to see their relationships nor to judge their differences; to perceive several objects separately from one another is not to number them. I can have at the same moment the idea of a large stick and of a small stick without comparing them, without judging that one is smaller than the other, as I can see at one time my whole hand without counting my fingers.[1] These comparative ideas, *greater, smaller,* as the numerical ideas of *one, two,* etc., are certainly not sensations, though my mind produces them only as a consequence of my sensations.

They tell us that the sensitive being distinguishes sensations from one another by the differences which those sensations bear one to the other. This requires explanation. When the sensations are different, the sensitive being distinguishes them by their differences; when they are similar, it distinguishes them because it perceives them separately. Otherwise, in a simultaneous sensation, how would it distinguish two identical objects? Necessarily it would have to confuse those two objects and take them for the same one, especially in a system in which they claim that sensations representing extension do not in themselves have extension.

When the two sensations to be compared are perceived, their impression is produced, each object is perceived, the two together are perceived, but that does not

---

1 The papers of M. de la Condamine tell us of a people who knew how to count only up to three. Yet the men who made up this people, having hands, had often perceived their fingers, without knowing how to count to five.

mean that their relationship is perceived. If the judgment of this relationship were only a sensation, and came to me uniquely from the object, my judgments would never deceive me, since it is never false that I perceive what I perceive.

Judgment is the faculty of an active mind

Why then is it that I am mistaken about the relationship of these two sticks, especially if they are not parallel? Why do I say, for example, that the small stick is a third the size of the large one when it is only a quarter? Why is the image, which is the sensation, not in conformity with its model, which is the object? It is because I am the agent when I judge, the operation of making the comparison is at fault, and my understanding, which judges the relationships, mingles its errors with the truth of the sensations which show only the objects themselves.

Add to that a reflection which will strike you, I am sure, when you have thought of it: it is that if we were purely passive in the use of our senses, there would be no coördination between them; it would be impossible for us to know that the body which we touch and the object which we see are one and the same. Either we should never perceive anything outside ourselves, or there would be for us five perceptible substances, whose identity we should have no means of recognizing.

When you give such or such a name to this power of my mind which brings together and compares my sensations—whether you call it attention, meditation, reflection, or what you will—it is always true that it is in me and not in the things, that it is I alone who produce it, although I produce it only when given the impression which the objects make upon me. Without being master of perceiving or not perceiving, I am master of examining in greater or less degree what I perceive.

I am not, then, merely a sensitive and passive being, but an active and intelligent one; and, whatever philosophy may say, I shall dare to claim the honor of thinking. I know only that the truth is in things and not in my mind which judges them, and that the less I put of my own in the judgments that I make concerning them, the surer I am of approaching the truth: thus my rule of trusting feeling more than reason is confirmed by reason itself.

Qualities of matter deduced from sense perceptions

Having thus so to speak assured myself of my own being, I begin to look outside myself, and I observe myself, with a sort of shudder, cast out, lost in this vast universe, and as it were swallowed up in the immensity of beings, without knowing anything of what they are either in an absolute sense, or in relation to one another, or in relation to me. I study them, I observe them; and the first object which is offered me for purposes of comparison is myself.

All that I perceive through the senses is matter, and I deduce all the essential properties of matter from the sensible qualities which make me perceive it, and which are inseparable from it. I see it sometimes in movement and sometimes at rest[2]; from that I infer that neither rest nor movement is essential to it, but movement being an action is the effect of a cause of which rest is only the absence. When, then, nothing acts on matter, it does not move, and for this very reason that it is indifferent to rest and to movement, its natural state must be to be at rest.

Communicated movement in lifeless matter; spontaneous movement in living beings

I perceive in bodies two sorts of movement, namely communicated movement, and spontaneous or voluntary movement. In the first, the cause of movement is outside the body moved, and in the second it is within it. I shall not conclude from that that the movement of a

2 This rest is, if you wish, only relative; but since we observe degrees in movement, we conceive very clearly one of the two extreme terms, which is rest; and we conceive it so clearly that we are even inclined to consider as absolute the rest which is only relative. Now it is not true that movement is of the essence of matter if matter can be conceived as being at rest.

watch, for example, is spontaneous, for if nothing outside the spring acted on it, it would not tend to straighten out and would not activate the train of gears. For the same reason, I shall not accord spontaneity to fluids either, nor even to the fire which causes their fluidity.[3]

You will ask me whether the movements of animals are spontaneous; I shall tell you that I know nothing about it, but that analogy indicates an affirmative answer. You will ask me how I know then that there are spontaneous movements; I shall tell you that I know it because I feel it. I wish to move my arm, and I move it, without that movement having any other immediate cause than my will. It is in vain that one should seek to argue in order to destroy in me that feeling, for it is stronger than any proofs; one might just as well seek to prove to me that I do not exist.

If there were no spontaneity in the actions of men, nor in anything that is done on earth, we should then be all the more perplexed to imagine the first cause of all movement. As far as I am concerned, I feel so convinced that the natural state of matter is to be at rest, and that it has in itself no force to act, that when I see a body in movement I judge immediately either that it is an animate body, or that this movement was communicated to it. My mind refuses any acceptance of the idea of non-organized matter moving by itself or producing any action.

A cause outside the physical universe produces its movement
And yet this visible universe is matter, matter dispersed and inert,[4] which has in its total mass nothing of the unity, the organization, the common feeling of

---

[3] Chemists regard phlogiston, or the element of fire, as diffused, motionless and stagnant in mixed bodies of which it is a part, until outside causes free it, bring it together, set it in motion, and change it into fire.

[4] I have made many efforts to conceive of a living molecule, without being able to achieve it. The idea of matter feeling without having senses seems to me unintelligible and contradictory. To adopt or to reject this idea it would first be necessary to understand it, and I confess that I do not have that good fortune.

the parts of an animate body, since it is certain that we who are parts have no perception of belonging to a vast whole. This same universe is in movement, and in its movements—controlled, uniform, subject to constant laws—it has nothing of that liberty which appears in the spontaneous movements of man and animals. The world is not, then, a great animal which moves by itself; there is, then, for its movements some cause outside itself which I do not perceive; but deep within myself I feel keenly that that cause does exist; so much so that I cannot see the sun advance in its course without imagining a force driving it, or that, if the earth revolves, I think I am aware of a hand which turns it.

If it is necessary to admit general laws, whose essential relationships with matter I do not perceive, what will they avail me? Those laws not being real entities, substances, have then some other basis which is unknown to me. Experience and observation have made us aware of the laws of motion; those laws govern the effects without revealing the causes; they are not sufficient to explain the system of the world and the operation of the universe. Descartes sought to explain the formation of heaven and earth on the basis of a throw of dice, but he could not set those dice in motion, nor bring into play his centrifugal force, except with the help of a movement of rotation. Newton discovered the law of gravitation; but gravitation alone would soon reduce the universe to a motionless mass: to that law he had to add a propulsive force to make the heavenly bodies advance on their elliptical orbits. Let Newton show us the hand which launched the planets on the tangent of their orbits.

The first causes of movement are not in matter; it receives movement and communicates it, but it does not produce it. The more I observe the action and reaction of the forces of nature acting on one another, the more I find that, along a chain of effects, one must always go back to some will for the first cause; for to suppose an infinite series of causes is to suppose none at all. In a word, any movement which is not produced by another can be the product only of a spontaneous, willful act; inanimate bodies act only by movement, and there is no real action without will. That is my first principle. I think then that a will moves the universe and animates nature. That is my first dogma, or my first article of faith.

Mysterious relationship of body and spirit
How can a will produce a physical and corporal action? I know nothing about it, but I feel within myself that it does produce it. I want to act, and I act; I want to move my body, and my body moves; but that a body without life and at rest should happen to move by itself or produce movement, that is incomprehensible and without example. The will is known to me by its acts, not by its nature. I know that will as a cause of movement; but to conceive of matter producing movement is clearly to imagine an effect without a cause; it is to imagine nothing at all.

It is no more possible for me to conceive how my own will moves my body than to conceive how my sensations affect my spirit. I don't even know why one of these mysteries has seemed more explicable than the other. For myself, either when I am passive or when I am active, the mode of union of the two substances seems to me absolutely incomprehensible. It is indeed strange that one should take this very incomprehensibility as a starting point to arrive at an identification of the two substances, as if operations of such a different nature were better explained in a single subject than in two.

The dogma which I have just established is obscure, it is true, but in any event it makes sense, and there is nothing in it which reason or observation repudiates; can one say as much of materialism? Is it not clear that if movement were of the essence of matter, it would be inseparable from it, it would always be present in matter in

14

the same degree, always the same in each portion of matter; it would be incommunicable, it could neither increase nor diminish, and one could not even imagine matter at rest? When I am told that movement is not essential to matter, but is necessary, someone is trying to fool me with words which would be easier to refute if they had a little more sense: for either the movement of matter comes to it from itself, and then it is essential to it, or if it comes to it from an outside cause, it is necessary to matter only in so far as the moving cause acts upon it—and that brings us back to the first difficulty.

Absurdities of metaphysics General and abstract ideas are the source of the greatest errors of men; never has the jargon of metaphysics led to the discovery of a single truth, and it has filled philosophy with absurdities of which one is ashamed as soon as one has stripped them of their high-sounding words. Tell me, my friend, if when they speak to you about a blind force permeating all nature they convey some real idea to your mind. People think they are saying something when they use these vague terms of universal force, of necessary movement—and they are saying nothing at all. The idea of movement is nothing other than the idea of transporting from one place to another: there is no movement without some direction, for a single being could not move at once in all directions. In what direction, then, does matter necessarily move? Does all the matter in a body have a uniform movement, or does each atom have its own movement? According to the first idea, the whole universe must form a solid and indivisible mass; according to the second, it must form only a diffuse and incoherent fluid without any possibility of two atoms ever coming together. In what direction will this common movement of all matter take place? Will it be in a straight line or in a circle, upwards or downwards, to right or to left? If each molecule of matter has its own direction, what will be the causes of all these directions and of all these differences? If each atom or molecule of matter merely revolved about its own center, nothing would ever leave its place, and no movement would ever be communicated; even so, this circular movement would have to be determined in some direction. To attribute to matter movement by abstraction is to use words that mean nothing; and to attribute to it a determined movement is to suppose a cause which determines it. The more I multiply individual forces, the more new causes I have to explain, without ever finding any common agent who directs them. Far from being able to imagine any order in the fortuitous concourse of the elements, I can't even imagine their combat, and the chaos of the universe is to me more inconceivable than its harmony. I realize that the mechanism of the world cannot be intelligible to the human mind; but as soon as a man undertakes to explain it, he must say things which men understand.

Divine intelligence governs universe
If the movement of matter reveals to me a will, the movement of matter according to certain laws reveals to me an intelligence; that is my second article of faith. Acting, comparing, choosing, these are the operations of an active and thinking being: therefore that being exists. "Where do you see him?" you are going to ask me. Not only in the revolving heavens, in the sun which gives us light; not only in myself, but in the grazing sheep, the flying bird, the falling stone, the leaf borne away by the wind.

I recognize the order of the world though I know not the purpose of it, because to recognize that order it suffices for me to compare its parts one with the other, to study the pattern by which they fit together, to note their relationships, to observe their harmony. I do not know why the universe exists; but I do not fail to see how it is modified; I do not fail to perceive the intimate correspondence by which the beings who compose it lend one another a mutual help. I am like a man who should see, for the first time, the movement of a watch, and who would not fail to admire the workmanship, although he did not know the use of the machine and he had not seen the dial. I do not know, he would say, what the purpose of the whole thing is, but I see that each part is formed to work in unison with the others: I admire the workman in the detail of his work, and I am quite sure that all the cogs run thus in harmony only for a common end which it is impossible for me to perceive.

Order is not the product of chance
Let us compare the individual ends, the means, the ordered relationships of every sort, then let us listen to our inner voice: what sound mind can deny its testimony? To what unprejudiced eyes does the perceptible order of the universe not announce a supreme intelligence? And how many sophisms must be accumulated so that one may fail to recognize the harmony of beings and the admirable contribution of each part toward the conservation of the others! Talk to me all you will of combinations and chances: what is the use of reducing me to silence if you cannot succeed in persuading me? And how will you take from me the involuntary feeling which, in spite of myself, always declares you wrong? If organized bodies were combined by chance in a thousand ways before assuming constant forms, if there were formed first stomachs without mouths, feet without heads, hands without arms, imperfect organs of every sort which have perished because they were incapable of enduring, why do we observe none of these formless productions today? Why has nature finally set for herself laws to which at first she was not subject? I must not be surprised that a thing should happen when it is possible and when the improbability of the event is counterbalanced by the great number of attempts; this I freely admit. And yet if you should come and tell me that printer's type, thrown down at random, formed the text of the Aeneid all ar-

ranged in order, I'd not deign to take a step to go and verify the falsehood. You forget, you will tell me, the number of possible chances. But of those chances, how many must I suppose in order to make the combination plausible? So far as I am concerned, I see only one possibility: the odds are infinity to one that the product of the combination is not the result of chance. Consider also that combinations and chances will never give products of a different nature from that of the elements combined, that organization and life will not result from the chance coming together of atoms, and that a chemist combining compounds will not make them feel and think in his crucible.[5]

I have read Nieuwentit* with surprise and almost with a feeling of scandal. How could this man have dared make a book of the marvels of nature, which reveal the wisdom of its creator? Were his book as big as the world, he would not have exhausted his subject; and as soon as one seeks to enter into details, the greatest marvel of all eludes one, and that is the harmony and concord of the whole. The mere generation of living and organized bodies is an utter mystery to the human mind; the insurmountable barrier which nature has set between the various species, so that they may not be crossed, reveals her intentions with the utmost clarity. It was not enough for her to establish order; she took sure measures to guarantee that nothing could disturb that order.

5 Would one believe, if one did not have proof of it, that human folly could be carried so far? Amatus Lusitanus declared that he had seen enclosed in a glass a little man an inch long whom Julius Camillus, like a second Prometheus, had produced by alchemy. Paracelsis, in *De natura rerum*, teaches the way of producing these little men, and maintains that pygmies, fauns, satyrs and nymphs have been engendered by chemistry. Indeed, I do not see too well what more remains to be done to establish the possibility of these facts than to maintain that organic matter resists burning by fire, and that its molecules can be kept alive in a reverberatory furnace.

*Bernard Nieuwentit, 1654-1729, Dutch mathematician and physician. The work to which Rousseau refers is titled *The Right Use of the Contemplation of the World*, 1715. [Translator's note]

There is not a being in the universe that one cannot regard in some respects as the common center of all others, about which they are all placed, in such a way that they are all mutually both ends and means to one another. The mind is confused and lost in this infinity of relationships, not one of which is confused or lost in the vast number. How many absurd suppositions have been made to deduce all this harmony from the blind mechanism of nature put into motion by chance! Those who deny the unity of intention which is manifest in the relationships of all the parts of this great whole cover in vain their gibberish with abstractions, coördinations, general principles, symbolic terms; whatever they may do, it is impossible for me to conceive a system of beings so constantly regulated without my conceiving an intelligence which governs it. I am not capable of believing that passive and inert matter could produce living and sentient beings, that a blind fatality could produce intelligent beings, that what does not think could produce thinking beings.

I believe, then, that the world is governed by a powerful and wise will; I see it, or rather I feel it, and that is important for me to know. But is this same world eternal or created? Is there a single source of things? Are there two, or several? And what is their nature? Of that I know nothing, and what difference does it make to me? As I grow more interested in this knowledge, I shall seek to acquire it; until then I shall not concern myself with idle questions which may disturb my pride but which are useless for my conduct and beyond the grasp of my reason.

God the being who governs all things Remember always that I am not teaching what I believe, I am merely setting it forth. Whether matter be eternal or created, whether there be a passive principle or not, still it is certain that the whole is one and reveals a single intelligence— for I see nothing which does not have its place in the same well-ordered system, and which does not contribute to the same end, namely the preservation of the whole in the established order. This being who has will and power, this being active in himself, this being finally, whatever he may be, who moves the universe and governs all things, I call him God. I associate with that name the ideas of intelligence, of power, of will which I have brought together, and that of goodness which is a necessary consequence of them; but that does not make me know better the being to whom I have attributed it. He eludes both my senses and my intelligence. The more I ponder over this, the more confused I become, but I do know most certainly that he exists, and that he exists by himself; I know that my existence is subordinated to his, and that all things which are known to me depend on him also. I perceive God everywhere in his works; I feel him within me; I see him all about me; but as soon as I seek to contemplate him in himself, as soon as I wish to seek where he is, what he is, what is his substance, he escapes me and my troubled mind perceives nothing more.

Futility of reasoning about God's nature Filled with the feeling of my inadequacy, I shall never reason about the nature of God, unless I am obliged to do so by the feeling of his relationship to me. Such reasonings are always rash; a wise man should fear to undertake them, sure that he is not made to plumb these mysteries: for what is most insulting to the divinity is not to abstain from thinking about him, but to be wrong in one's thinking about him.

Man the king of nature After discovering those of his attributes by which I conceive his existence, I come back to myself, and I seek what place I occupy in the order of things which he governs, and which I can examine. I find myself incontestably in the first rank by virtue of my belonging to the human race; for by my will and by the instruments which are at my disposal to fulfill it, I am more capable of acting on all the bodies which surround me, whether to re-

20

ceive or to avoid their action as I may wish, than any of them are to act on me in spite of myself by mere physical impulsion; and, by my intelligence, I am the only one who can survey the whole. What being here below, apart from man, can observe all the others, measure, calculate, foresee their movements, their effects, and unite, as it were, the feeling of common existence to that of his own individual existence? What is so ridiculous about believing that everything is made for me, if I am the only one who knows how to consider everything in relation to himself?

It is therefore true that man is the king of nature, at least on this earth where he dwells; for not only does he master all the animals, not only does he make use of the elements by his industry, but he alone on earth can thus make use of them, and he even makes his own, by contemplation, the very stars which he cannot approach. Show me another animal on earth who knows how to use fire, and who knows how to admire the sun. What! I can observe and know beings and their relationships; I can feel what order, beauty, and virtue are; I can contemplate the universe, raise myself toward the hand which governs it; I can love good, and do good; and I should compare myself to the beasts? Abject soul, it is your wretched philosophy which makes you resemble them; or rather, you seek in vain to debase yourself: your genius reveals the error of your principles, your beneficent heart belies your doctrine, and the very abuse of your faculties proves their excellence in spite of you.

As for myself, who have no system to defend, a simple and honest man whom the zeal of no party leads astray and who does not aspire to the honor of being the leader of a school, content with the place to which God has assigned me, I see nothing beneath him better than the species to which I belong. If I had to choose my place in the order of beings, what more could I choose than to be a man?

Gratitude toward God
Rather than making me proud, this reflection

moves me deeply; for the state is not of my own choosing, and it was not due to the merit of a being who did not yet exist. Can I see myself thus distinguished without congratulating myself on occupying this honorable place, and without blessing the hand which put me there? Out of this preliminary self-examination there is born in my heart a feeling of gratitude and benediction toward the creator of mankind, and out of that feeling my first homage to the beneficent deity. I adore the supreme power, and its favors move me deeply. There is no need to teach me this worship; it is dictated by nature itself. Is it not a natural consequence of our instinct for self-preservation to honor what protects us and to love what seeks our good?

Confusion in human society But when seeking later my individual place within the human species, I consider its organization, the various ranks and the men who occupy them, what becomes of me? What a spectacle! Where is the order which I had observed? The spectacle of nature offered me only harmony and proportions; that of mankind offers me only confusion and disorder! Harmony prevails among the elements, and men are in chaos! Animals are happy; their king alone is wretched! O wisdom, where are thy laws? O providence, is it thus that thou dost govern the world? Beneficent being, what has become of thy power? I see evil on this earth.

Conflict of reason and passions Would you believe, my good friend, that out of these sad reflections and these apparent contradictions there took shape in my mind the sublime ideas of the soul, which had not heretofore emerged from my pursuit of truth? While meditating upon the nature of man, I thought I discovered in it two distinct principles, one of which raised him to the study of eternal truths, to the love of justice and the moral good, to the regions of the intellectual world whose contemplation constitutes the delight of the sage, and the other of

22

which brought him down basely into himself, made him a slave to the empire of the senses, to the passions which are their ministers, and opposed by those passions all the noble and great aspirations inspired in him by the recognition of the former principle. Feeling myself carried away, drawn into conflict by these two contrary movements, I said to myself: No, man is not one; I will, and I do not will, I feel myself at the same time slave and free; I see the good, I love it, and yet I do evil; I am active when I listen to reason, passive when my passions lead me astray; and my worst torment, when I yield, is to feel that I might have resisted.

Dual nature of man

Young man, listen with confidence, for I shall always speak to you in good faith. If conscience is the product of prejudices, I am doubtless wrong, and there is no proven morality; but if to place oneself above everything is a natural inclination in man, and if, nonetheless, the first sentiment of justice is inborn in the human heart, then let him who considers man a simple being explain away these contradictions, and I shall recognize henceforth only one substance.

You will note that by this term *substance* I mean in general the being endowed with some primitive quality, disregarding individual or secondary modifications. If, then, all the primitive qualities which are known to us can be brought together in a single being, one must admit only one substance; but if there are some which are mutually exclusive, there are as many various substances as there are such exclusions. You will reflect on that; for myself, whatever Locke may say, I need only know matter as having extent and being divisible to be assured that it cannot think; and when a philosopher comes along to tell me that trees feel and rocks think,[6] it will be useless for him to entangle me in his subtle arguments. It is impossible for me to see in him anything but a sophist of bad faith, who prefers to attribute feeling to stones rather than grant a soul to man.

Let us suppose a deaf man who denies the existence of sounds because they have never struck his ear. I place before his eyes a stringed instrument, which I make vibrate in unison with a hidden instrument; the deaf man sees the cord tremble; I say to him: "It is the sound which does that." "Not at all," he answers; "the cause of the vibration of the cord is in itself; it is a quality common to all bodies to vibrate in this way." "Show me then," I go on, "that trembling in other bodies, or at least its cause in this string." "I cannot," answers the deaf man; "but because I do not conceive how that string vibrates, why should I go and explain that by your sounds, of which I don't have the slightest idea? That is explaining an obscure fact by an even more obscure cause. Either

6 It seems to me that far from saying that rocks think, modern philosophy has discovered on the contrary that men do not think. It no longer recognizes any but sensitive beings in nature; and the only difference it finds between a man and a stone is that the man is a sensitive being who has sensations, and the stone a sensitive being who has none. But if it is true that all matter feels, where shall I conceive the sensitive unity or the individual self? Will it be in each molecule of matter, or in aggregate bodies? Shall I attribute equally this unity to fluids and to solids, to compounds and to elements? There are, they say, only individuals in nature! But what are these individuals? Is this stone an individual, or an aggregation of individuals? Is it a single sensitive being, or is each constituent grain of sand one? If each elementary atom is a sensitive being, how shall I conceive that intimate communication by which one feels itself within the other, so that their two selves are merged in one? Attraction may be a law of nature whose mystery is unknown to us; but we conceive at least that attraction, operating according to masses, is in no wise incompatible with extension and divisibility. Do you conceive the same thing with respect to feeling? The sensitive parts have extension, but the sensitive being is indivisible and one; it cannot be divided; it is quite entire, or it does not exist— the sensitive being is not, therefore, a body. I don't know how our materialists understand it, but it seems to me that the same difficulties which have made them reject thought ought to make them also reject feeling; and I don't see why, after taking the first step, they should not take the second also: what more would it cost them? And since they are sure that they do not think, how do they dare affirm that they feel?

24

make me perceive your sounds, or I'll continue to say they don't exist."

The more I reflect on thought and on the nature of the human mind, the more convinced I am that the reasoning of the materialists resembles that of this deaf man. They are deaf, indeed, to the inner voice which calls out to them in a tone which can scarcely be ignored: "A machine does not think, there is no movement or form which produces reflection; something within you seeks to break the bonds which confine it; space is not your measure, the whole universe is not big enough for you, your feelings, your desires, your anxiety, your very pride, have a different principle from this small body in which you feel yourself imprisoned."

No merely material entity is active in itself, and I am. There is no use arguing with me about that, I feel it, and that feeling which speaks to me is stronger than the reason which combats it. I have a body on which others act, and which acts on them; that reciprocal action is not to be doubted. At the same time my will is independent of my senses, and I consent or I resist, I succumb or I prevail, and I feel distinctly within myself when I do what I have willed to do, or when I only yield to my passions. I have always the strength to will, but not always the strength to carry out my will. When I yield to temptations, I act according to the impulsion of external objects. When I reproach myself with that weakness, I listen only to my will. I am a slave by my vices, and free by my remorse; the feeling of my liberty is effaced in me when I am depraved, and I prevent finally the voice of the soul from rising against the law of the body.

Man's freedom of will proves existence of his soul

I know what the will is only through experiencing my own will, and what the understanding is, is no better known to me. When I am asked what the cause is which determines my will, I ask in my turn what the cause is which determines my judgment. It is clear that these two causes are only one; and if you understand clearly that man is active in his judgments, that his understanding is only the power of comparing and judging, you will see that his liberty is nothing other than a comparable power, or that it is derived from that one—he chooses the good as he has judged the true; if he judges ill, he chooses ill. What is the cause which determines his judgment? It is his intelligent faculty, it is his power of judging; the determining cause is within himself. Beyond that, I understand nothing more.

Doubtless I am not free not to will my own good, I am not free to will harm to myself; but my liberty consists precisely in this fact that I can will only what is suitable for me, or what I consider to be so, without anything outside myself determining my choice. Does it follow that I am not my master because I am not master of being someone other than myself?

The spring of all action is in the will of a free being, one cannot go back farther than that. It is not the word *liberty* which is meaningless, it is *necessity*. To suppose some act, some effect which does not derive from an active principle is really to suppose effects without cause; it is to fall into the vicious circle. Either there is no first impulse, or every first impulse has no previous cause, and there is no real will without liberty. Man is therefore free in his actions, and as such animated by an immaterial substance; this is my third article of faith. From these first three, you will readily deduce all the others without my continuing to enumerate them.

Man's power to do evil a part of his superiority
If man is active and free, he is responsible for his acts; all that he does freely does not enter into the ordered system of Providence, and cannot be imputed to it. God does not will the evil which man commits in abusing the liberty which has been given him, but God does not prevent man's committing it,

26

either because on the part of so weak a creature this evil is as nothing in his eyes, or because he could not prevent it without limiting man's liberty and doing a greater evil by degrading his nature. God has made him free so that he might do, not evil, but good, by choice. He put man in a position to make this choice by using properly the faculties with which he is endowed; but he so limited his powers that the abuse of the liberty which God leaves to man cannot disturb the general order. The evil that man does affects him without changing anything in the system of the world, without preventing mankind from being preserved in spite of itself. To protest because God does not prevent man from doing evil is to protest against his having endowed him with an excellent nature, against his having placed over his actions the morality which ennobles them, against his having given man the right to virtue. The supreme enjoyment is in satisfaction with oneself; it is to merit this satisfaction that we are placed on earth and endowed with liberty, that we are tempted by passions and restrained by conscience. What more could the divine power itself do in our favor? Could it establish a contradiction in our nature and reward for doing good a being who had no power to do evil? What! to keep man from being wicked, should he have been limited to instinct and reduced to the level of a beast? No, God of my soul, I shall never protest against thy making man in thy image, so that I may be free, good and happy like thee!

We create the woes which afflict us
It is the abuse of our faculties which makes us unhappy and wicked. Our griefs, our cares, our troubles, come to us from ourselves. Moral evil is incontestably our work, and physical woes would be nothing without our vices which have brought them on us. Is it not for our own preservation that nature has made us feel our needs? Is not physical pain a sign that the machine is out of order, and a warning to attend

27

to it? Death. . . Do the wicked not poison their own life and ours? Who would want to live always among them? Death is the remedy for the ills you bring upon yourself; nature has willed that you should not suffer for ever. To what few ills is subject the man who lives in primitive simplicity! He lives almost without maladies as without passions, and neither foresees nor feels death; when he does feel it, his sufferings make it desirable to him: henceforth it is no longer an evil for him. If we were satisfied with being what we are, we should not have to deplore our fate; but, in order to seek an imaginary well-being, we give ourselves a thousand real ills. He who cannot endure a little suffering must expect to suffer a great deal. When you have ruined your constitution by a life of excesses, you seek to rebuild it with remedies. To the misfortune you are undergoing, you add the one you fear. Foreseeing death makes it appear horrible and speeds its coming; the more you seek to flee it, the closer you feel it; and you are dying of fear throughout your whole life, while blaming nature for the ills which you have brought on yourself by offending nature.

Man is the author of evil   Man, seek no more the author of evil; that author is yourself. There exists no other evil than the evil you do or you suffer, and both come from you. General evil can exist only in disorder, and I see in the system of the world an order which in no wise belies itself. Individual evil is only in the feeling of the being who suffers; and man has not received this feeling from nature; he has given it to himself. Suffering has little hold on him who, having reflected little, has neither memory nor fear. Take away our ill-fated progress, take away our errors and our vices, take away the work of man, and all is well.

God is all-powerful and all-good   Where all is well nothing is unjust. Justice is inseparable from goodness. Now goodness is the necessary effect of a limitless power

28

and of the desire for one's own well-being which is of the essence of any being aware of his own existence. He who can do all things extends, so to speak, his existence to include the existence of all creatures. The perpetual action of power is to produce and to preserve. It does not act upon what is not. God is not the god of the dead, he could not be destructive and malicious without harming himself. He who can do all can will only what is good.[7] Therefore the sovereignly good Being, because he is sovereignly powerful, must be also sovereignly just; otherwise he would contradict himself, for the love of order which produces order is called *goodness*, and the love of order which preserves it is called *justice*.

Happiness results from justice

God, they say, owes nothing to his creatures. I believe that he owes them everything he promised them by giving them life. Now to give them the idea of a good and to make them feel the need of it is to promise it to them. The more I explore my own consciousness, and the more I study myself, the more I read these words written in my soul: *Be just, and you will be happy*. And yet this is not at all so if you consider the present state of things; the wicked man prospers, and the just remains oppressed. See also what indignation is aroused within us when this expectation is not fulfilled! Conscience rises and protests against its creator; it cries out in a moan: Thou hast deceived me!

How do you know, rash one, that I have deceived you? Is your soul utterly destroyed? Have you ceased to exist? O Brutus! O my son! Do not sully your noble life by ending it; do not leave your hope and your glory upon the field of Philippi. Why do you say "virtue is nothing," when you are about to enjoy the reward of your virtue?

7 When the ancients called the supreme God *optimus maximus* (most good and most great) they were using a quite true term; but by saying *maximus optimus* (most great and most good) they would have spoken more exactly. God is good because he is great.

You are going to die, you think: no, you are going to live, and it is then that I shall fulfill all I have promised you.

One would think, by the murmurs of impatient mortals, that God owes them the reward before they have demonstrated their merit, and that he is obliged to pay in advance for their virtue. Oh! Let us be good first, and then we shall be happy. Let us not demand the prize before the victory, nor the wages before the work. It is not in the lists, said Plutarch, that the champions in our sacred games are crowned, it is after they have emerged from the contests.

Soul survives the body, and may be presumed immortal   If the soul is immaterial, it can survive the body; if the soul does survive it, Providence is justified. Even if I had no other proof of the immaterial nature of the soul than the triumph of the wicked and the oppression of the just in this world, that alone would prevent me from doubting it. So manifest a contradiction, so shocking a dissonance in the universal harmony, would make me seek an explanation. I should say to myself: Everything does not end for us with this life; at death, everything goes back into order. I should have, it is true, the problem of asking myself where man is when everything of his physical being is destroyed. This question is no longer a difficulty for me so soon as I have recognized two substances. It is obvious that, during my bodily life, perceiving nothing except through my senses, what is not of their domain eludes me. When the union of the body and the soul is broken, I conceive that one can be dissolved and the other preserved. Why should the destruction of one entail the destruction of the other? On the contrary, being of such different natures, they were, by their union, in a violent state; and when that union ceases, they both return to their natural state: the active and living substance regains all the force it used in moving the passive and inert substance. Alas! I feel it too well by my own vices, man only half lives during his life, and the life of the soul begins only with the death of the body.

But what is that life? and is the soul immortal by its nature? I do not know. My limited understanding conceives nothing without limits; everything they call infinite is beyond me. What can I deny, affirm? What reasonings can I pursue concerning what I cannot conceive? I believe that the soul survives the body sufficiently to assure the divine order: who knows if it is enough to live forever? However, I conceive how the body is worn out and destroyed by the division of its parts, but I cannot conceive a similar destruction of the thinking being; and, not imagining how it can die, I presume that it does not die. Since that presumption consoles me, and is in no way unreasonable, why should I fear to accept it?

Recollections of a virtuous life make the soul happy

I feel my soul, I know it by feeling and by thought; I know what it is, without knowing what its essence is; I cannot reason about ideas which I do not have. What I do know well is that the identity of the self is prolonged only by memory, and that, to be indeed the same person I was, I must remember having been. Now I cannot recall after my death what I have been during my life unless I remember also what I have felt, consequently what I have done; and I doubt not that one day this memory will be the source of the happiness of the good and the torment of the wicked. Here below a thousand burning passions absorb our inner being and mask remorse. The humiliations, the disgrace which the practice of virtues draws upon us, prevent our feeling all their charms. But when, freed of the illusions that body and senses burden us with, we shall enjoy the contemplation of the supreme Being and of the eternal truths of which he is the source, when the beauty of order will strike all the faculties of our soul, and when we shall be uniquely occupied in comparing what we have done with what we ought to have done, it is then that the voice

31

of conscience will recapture its strength and its power; it is then that the pure pleasure which is born of self-content, and the bitter regret of having debased oneself, will distinguish by inexhaustible sentiments the fate that each will have prepared for himself. Do not ask me, O my good friend, whether there will be other sources of happiness and of griefs; I do not know. Those I imagine are enough to console me for this life and to make me hope for another. I do not say that the good will be rewarded, for what other good can an excellent being expect than to exist according to its nature? but I say that they will be happy, because their creator, the author of all justice, having made them sensitive, did not make them for suffering. I further say that, not having abused their liberty on earth, they have not by their fault lost their goal; they have, however, suffered in this life—they will then find compensation in another. This feeling is founded less upon the merit of man than upon the notion of goodness which seems to me inseparable from the divine essence. I am only supposing the laws of order carried out, and God consistent with himself.

Punishment of sin occurs in this life

Don't ask me either whether the torments of the wicked will be eternal, and whether the goodness of the author of their being can condemn them to suffer for ever. Again, I do not know, and I do not have the vain curiosity to explore useless questions. What does it matter to me what will become of the wicked? I take little interest in their fate. And yet I find it hard to believe that they will be condemned to endless torments. If the supreme justice is vengeful, it takes vengeance in this life. You and your errors, O nations, are its ministers. It employs the woes you make for yourselves to punish the crimes which have drawn them on you. It is in your insatiable hearts, eaten with envy, avarice and ambition, that in the midst of your false prosperity the avenging passions punish your crimes. What need is there to go to seek hell in the other life? It is already in this life in the heart of the wicked.

Where our perishable needs end, where our mad desires cease, there must cease also our passions and our crimes. Of what perversity would pure spirits be capable? Having need of nothing, why should they be wicked? If, deprived of our vulgar senses, all their happiness is in the contemplation of beings, they can will only good; and he who ceases to be wicked, can he be forever wretched? That's what I'm inclined to believe, without taking the trouble to come to a definite decision on the subject. O clement and good Being! whatever thy decrees may be, I adore them. If thou dost punish eternally the wicked, my feeble reason submits before your justice; but if the remorse of those unfortunate ones is to be dulled with time, if their woes are to end, and if the same peace awaits us all equally one day, I praise thee for that reason. Is the wicked man not my brother? How many times have I been tempted to resemble him! If, freed from his misery, he should lose also the curse which accompanies him, if he should be happy as I, far from arousing my jealousy, his happiness will only add to mine.

God is beyond our comprehension, but many of his attributes are clear

It is thus that, contemplating God in his works and studying him by those of his attributes which it was important for me to know, I succeeded in extending and augmenting by degrees the idea, at first imperfect and limited, which I had of that immense Being. But if that idea has become progressively more noble and great, it has also grown beyond the proportions which the human reason can grasp. As I approach in spirit the eternal light, its brilliance dazzles me, disturbs me, and I am forced to abandon all the earthly notions which helped me to imagine him. God is no longer corporeal and perceptible to my senses; the supreme intelligence which governs the world is no longer the world itself; I lift my mind in vain and weary it seeking to conceive his inconceivable essence. When the idea comes to me that it is that essence which gives life and activity to the living and active substance which governs animate bodies, when I hear that my soul is spiritual and that God is a spirit, then I grow indignant against such a debasement of the divine essence. As if God and my soul were of the same nature! As if God were not the only absolute being, the only being really active, feeling, thinking, willing by himself, and through whom we possess thought, feeling, activity, will, liberty, being! We are free only because he wants us to be free, and his inexplicable substance is to our souls what our souls are to our bodies. Whether he has created matter, bodies, minds, the world, I do not know at all. The idea of creation confounds me, and passes my understanding; I believe in it so far as I can conceive it. I know, however, that he has formed the universe and all that exists, that he has made everything, ordered everything. God is eternal, doubtless; but can my mind embrace the idea of eternity? Why should I dupe myself with words which convey no idea? What I conceive is that he is before things, that he will be so long as they persist, and that he would be even after them, if everything were to end one day. That a being beyond my comprehension should give existence to other beings, that is only obscure and incomprehensible; but that being and nothingness should be converted by themselves into one another, that is an obvious contradiction, that is a patent absurdity.

God is intelligent; but how is he intelligent? Man is intelligent when he reasons, and the supreme intelligence does not need to reason; there are for it neither premises nor conclusions, there are not even any propositions; it is purely intuitive, it sees equally all that is and all that can be; all truths are for it only a single idea, as all places a single point, and all times a single moment. Human power acts by means, divine power acts by itself. God can, because he wills; his will makes his power. God is good, nothing is more manifest; but goodness in man is the love of his fellows, and the goodness of God is the love of order, for it is by order that he maintains what exists, and links each part with the whole. God is just; I am convinced of it; it is a consequence of his goodness. The injustice of men is their work, and not his. Moral disorder, which testifies against Providence in the eyes of the philosophers, only demonstrates the existence of Providence to mine. But man's justice is to render unto each his due, and the justice of God is to ask of each an accounting of what he has given.

If I happen to discover one after another these attributes of which I have no absolute idea, it is by necessary consequences, it is by the good use of my reason; but I affirm them without understanding them, and, at bottom, that is affirming nothing. Even though I say to myself, God is thus, even though I feel it, even though I prove it to myself, yet I comprehend no better how God can be thus.

Finally, the more I strive to contemplate his infinite essence, the less I comprehend it; but it is, and that is enough for me—the less I comprehend it, the more I adore it. I feel humble, I say to him: "Being of beings, I am because thou art; to mediate unceasingly upon thee is to raise myself toward my source. The most worthy use of my reason is for it to be as nothing before thee: it is the delight of my spirit, it is the charm of my weakness, to feel myself overwhelmed by thy greatness."

Sure principles of conduct furnished by conscience From the impression of the objects I perceive and from the inner feeling which inclines me to judge causes according to my innate reason, having thus deduced the principal truths which it was important for me to know, there is left for me to seek what maxims I must draw from them to govern my conduct, and what rules I must prescribe for myself in order to fulfill my mission on earth according to the intention of him who placed me there. Still following my method, I do not draw these rules from the principles of a lofty philosophy, but I find them deep in my heart, written by nature in indelible characters. I have only to consult myself about what I wish to do: all that I feel to be good is good, all that I feel to be evil is evil. The best of all casuists is the conscience, and it is only when man seeks to strike a bargain with his conscience that he has recourse to the subtleties of reasoning. Man is concerned first of all with his own well-being: yet how many times the voice of conscience tells us that in serving our own interests at the expense of others we are doing wrong! We think we are following the voice of nature, and we resist it; listening to what she says to our senses, we disown what she says to our hearts—consequently the active being obeys, the passive being commands. Conscience is the voice of the soul, passions are the voice of the body. Is it astonishing that often these two tongues contradict one another? And then which should you heed? Too often reason deceives us; we have only too often acquired the right to challenge it. Conscience, on the contrary, never deceives us; it is the true guide of man; it is to the soul what instinct is to the body[8]; he who follows con-

8 Modern philosophy, which admits only what it explains, is careful not to admit this obscure faculty called instinct, which seems to guide, without any acquired knowledge, animals toward some end. Instinct, according to one of our wisest philosophers, is only a habit stripped of all reflection, but acquired through reflection; and, from the way in which he explains this progress, one must conclude that children reflect more than men—a paradox strange enough to merit its being examined. Without entering here into this discussion, I ask what name I am to give to the zeal with which my dog makes war on the moles which he does not eat, to the patience with which he lies in wait for whole hours sometimes, and to the skill with which he seizes them, pulls them out of the ground as soon as they make an appearance, and kills them afterwards and leaves them on the spot, without anyone ever training him for this hunt or teaching him that there were moles there. I ask also, and this is more important, why, the first time I threatened this same dog, he rolled over on his back, his paws drawn up in a supplicating attitude most fitting to move me; a posture in which he would have taken good care not to remain if I, without yielding to pity, had beaten him in that state. What! had

science obeys nature, and need not fear going astray. This point is important, my benefactor went on, seeing that I was going to interrupt him; let me stop a moment to throw more light on it.

Man is drawn to what is just and good

All the morality of our actions is in the judgment which we pass on them ourselves. If it is true that the good is good, it must be so deep in our hearts as in our works, and the first reward of justice is to feel that one is practicing it. If moral goodness is in conformity with our nature, man cannot be sound in spirit nor in constitution except in so far as he is good. If moral goodness is not in conformity with our nature, and if man is naturally wicked, he cannot cease being so without being corrupted, and goodness is in him only a vice against nature. Made to harm his fellow men as the wolf is made to slaughter his prey, a humane man would be as depraved as a wolf which shows pity; and virtue alone would leave us remorse.

Let us probe into ourselves, O my young friend! let us examine, setting aside all personal selfish considerations, to what our natural inclinations lead us. Which spectacle pleases us more, that of the torments or of the happiness of others? Which is more pleasant for us to perform, and leaves us afterwards with a more gratifying impression— an act of kindness or an act of maliciousness? For what character do you feel sympathy in a stage play? Do you take pleasure in crimes? Do you shed tears over the punishment of those who commit them? Everything is

my puppy, still quite small and only recently born, acquired moral ideas? Did he know what clemency and generosity are? On the basis of what acquired knowledge did he hope to appease me by abandoning himself in this way to my mercy? All the dogs in the world do approximately the same thing under similar circumstances, and I affirm nothing here that anyone cannot verify. Let the philosophers, who reject instinct so disdainfully, please explain this fact on the sole basis of sensations and of the knowledge which we acquire through sensations; let them explain it in such a manner as to satisfy any reasonable man—then I shall have nothing more to say, and I shall speak no more of instinct.

indifferent to us, they say, except our own self-interest; and, quite to the contrary, the pleasures of friendship, of humanity console us in our sorrows; and even in our pleasures, we should be too much alone, too wretched, if we did not have someone to share them with. If there is nothing moral in man's heart, whence come to him, then, those transports of admiration for heroic actions, those ardent feelings of love for great souls? What relationship does this enthusiasm for virtue have with our personal interest? Why should I wish to be Cato who disembowels himself rather than Caesar who triumphs? If you take from our hearts this love of the beautiful, you take away all the charm of life. He whose vile passions have stifled in his narrow soul these delightful sentiments, he who, by centering all his thoughts within himself, succeeds in having no love for anyone but himself, no longer has any thrill of emotion, his frozen heart no longer palpitates with joy, a gentle tenderness never moistens his eyes, he enjoys nothing any more; the unfortunate man no longer feels, no longer lives; he is already dead.

But, whatever may be the number of the wicked on earth, there are few of these cadaverous souls who have become insensitive, against their own interest, to everything which is just and good. Iniquity pleases only in so far as one profits by it; in all else, one wants the innocent to be protected. If we see in the street or along a road some act of violence or injustice, immediately a movement of anger and indignation rises from deep in our heart, and it inclines us to take the defense of the oppressed one; but a more powerful duty restrains us, and the laws take from us the right of protecting innocence. On the contrary, if some act of clemency or of generosity meets our eyes, what admiration, what love it inspires in us! Who is there who doesn't say to himself: I should like to have done as much? It is surely of little importance to us that two thousand years ago a man was wicked or just; and yet the events recorded in ancient history affect us as much as if they had taken place in our day. What do Catiline's crimes matter to me? Am I afraid of being his victim? Why then do I hold him in the same horror as if he were my contemporary? We do not hate the wicked merely because they may harm us, but because they are wicked. Not only do we wish to be happy, but we wish also the happiness of others; and when this happiness in no way harms our own, it adds to it. Finally, in spite of ourselves, we feel pity for the unfortunate; when we witness their trouble, we suffer with them. The most perverse cannot lose completely this inclination; often it produces a contradiction within them. The thief who robs passers-by still covers the nakedness of the poor; and the most fierce assassin supports a man falling in a faint.

Voice of remorse People often speak of the cry of remorse which punishes in secret hidden crimes, and brings them so often to light. Alas! who of us has never heard this importunate voice? They speak from experience; and we should like to stifle this tyrannical sentiment which torments us so much. Let us obey nature; we shall know how gently she reigns, and what delight we find, after listening to her, in proving our worth to ourselves. The wicked man fears himself, and seeks to flee himself; his pleasure lies in escaping from himself; he casts anxious looks about him, and seeks some object to amuse him; were it not for bitter satire, were it not for insulting mockery, he would always be sad; mocking laughter is his only pleasure. On the contrary, the serenity of the just man is an inner peace; his laughter is not maliciousness, but joy; he bears the source of that joy within himself; he is as gay alone as in the midst of friends; he does not draw his contentment from those who approach him, but he communicates it to them.

Man has an inborn principle of justice and virtue Cast your eyes over all the nations of the world, run through the histories of all peoples; among so many inhuman and strange cults, among that prodigious diversity of manners and characters, you will find everywhere the same ideas of justice and honesty, everywhere the same principles of morality, everywhere the same notions of good and evil. The paganism of antiquity gave birth to abominable gods whom one would have punished here below as rogues, and who offered as a picture of supreme happiness only crimes to be committed and passions to be satisfied. But vice, armed with a sacred authority, descended in vain from the eternal abode; the moral instinct repulsed it from the human heart. While celebrating the debauchery of Jupiter, one admired the continence of Xenocrates; chaste Lucretia worshipped the unchaste Venus; the intrepid Roman sacrificed to Fear; he invoked the god who mutilated his divine father, and he died without murmur at the hand of his own father. The most despicable divinities were served by the greatest men. The holy voice of nature, stronger than that of the gods, made itself respected on earth, and seemed to relegate to the abode of the gods crime and those guilty of it.

There is, then, deep in our souls an inborn principle of justice and virtue by which, in spite of our maxims, we judge our actions and those of others as good or bad; and it is to this principle that I give the name of conscience.

Examples of depravity do not disprove the general principle

But at the mention of this word, I hear rise from all sides the clamor of so-called wise men: Childish errors, prejudices derived from early upbringing! they all cry together. There is nothing in the human mind except what is introduced into it by experience, and we judge all things only according to acquired ideas. They go even farther; they dare to reject this obvious and universal accord of all nations, and, against the signal uniformity of the judgment of men, they go seeking in the darkness some obscure example known only to themselves; as if all the inclinations of nature were wiped out by the depravation of a single people, and as if, as soon as one discovers monsters, the race in general were no longer to be taken into account! But of what value to the skeptic Montaigne are the torments he gives himself by digging up in some corner of the world a custom opposed to the notions of justice? Of what avail is it to give to the most untrustworthy travelers the authority which he refuses the most untrustworthy writers? Will a few uncertain and strange practices, founded on local causes which are unknown to us, destroy the general deduction drawn from the common experience of all peoples, opposed to one another in everything else, and in agreement only on this single point? O Montaigne! you who pride yourself on frankness and truth, be sincere and true, if a philosopher can be so, and tell me if there is some land on earth where it is a crime to keep faith, to be merciful, beneficent, generous; where the man of honor is despised, and the perfidious man honored.

Self-interest inadequate to explain man's behavior — Each, they say, collaborates toward the public good for his own interest. But how does it happen, then, that the just man works for the public good at the cost of his own welfare? What does it mean to meet death for one's own interest? Doubtless none acts except for his own good; but if there is no moral good to be taken into account, one will never explain on the basis of self-interest any but the actions of the wicked—it is even to be believed that no attempt will be made to explain other actions. A philosophy in which virtuous actions would constitute an obstacle, in which the philosopher could justify himself only by inventing for them base intentions and motives without virtue, in which one would be obliged to debase Socrates and to calumniate Regulus, would be too abominable. If ever such doctrines could appear among us, the voice of nature, as well as the voice of reason, would rise immediately against them, and would never leave a single one of their partisans the excuse of believing their own doctrines in good faith.

41

My purpose is not to enter here into metaphysical discussions which are beyond my grasp and yours, and which, when all is said and done, lead to nothing. I have already told you that I didn't wish to philosophize with you, but to help you to examine your own inner consciousness. Even though all the philosophers in the world should prove that I am wrong, if you feel that I am right I ask nothing more.

Conscience based on innate feeling, not on acquired ideas.
To that end, I must merely show you the difference between our acquired ideas and our natural sentiments. We feel necessarily before knowing; and as we do not learn to wish for our good and to flee what is harmful to us, but as we receive that will from nature, so the love of good and the hatred of evil are as natural to us as self-love. The acts of conscience are not judgments, but feelings: although all our ideas come to us from outside, the feelings which weigh the worth of those ideas are within us, and it is by them alone that we know the suitability or unsuitability, so far as we are concerned, of the things which we must seek or avoid.

For us, to exist is to feel; our sensitivity incontestably comes before our intelligence, and we have feelings before ideas.[9] Whatever the cause of our being, it has provided for our preservation by giving us feelings suitable to our nature; and it cannot be denied that these at least are innate. These feelings, so far as the individual is concerned, are love of self, fear of pain, horror of death, de-

---

[9] In certain respects, ideas are feelings, and feelings are ideas. The two names are applicable to any perceptions which concern us both with the object of the perception, and with ourselves who are affected by it: there is only the order in which we are affected which determines the proper name. When, first of all occupied by the object, we think of ourselves only by reflection, it is an idea; on the contrary, when the impression received excites our attention first, and when we think only by reflection of the object which causes it, it is a feeling.

sire of well-being. But if, as we cannot doubt, man is sociable by his nature, or at least so formed that he may become sociable, he can be so only through other innate sentiments relative to his species; for considering only physical need, it must certainly disperse men rather than bring them together. Now it is from the moral system formed by this double relationship to himself and to his fellow men that the urge of conscience comes into being. To know the good is not to love it. Man does not have an innate knowledge of the good, but as soon as his reason makes him recognize it, his conscience moves him to love it; it is this sentiment which is inborn.

I do not believe, therefore, my friend, that it is impossible to explain by consequences of our nature the immediate source of conscience, independent of reason itself. And even if that were impossible, still it would not be necessary, since those who deny this principle, admitted and recognized by the whole human race, do not prove that it does not exist, but are content to affirm it. When we affirm that it does exist, our belief is just as well founded as theirs, and we have more testimony from within ourselves, and the voice of conscience which gives evidence in its own behalf. If the first glimmers of judgment dazzle us and in the beginning confuse before our eyes the objects which we view, let us wait until our weak eyes open again, grow stronger; and soon we shall see those same objects by the light of reason, as nature first revealed them to us—or rather, let us be more simple and less vain; let us limit ourselves to the first feelings which we find within ourselves, since it is always to them that study brings us back when it has not led us astray.

Conscience! conscience! divine instinct, immortal and celestial voice; sure guide of an ignorant and limited being, but intelligent and free; infallible judge of good and evil, who make man like God! it is you who make the excellence of his nature and the morality of his actions; without you, I feel nothing in me which raises me above the beasts, except the sad privilege of wandering from error to error with the help of an unguided understanding and an unprincipled reason.

Influences which stifle conscience

Thank heaven, here we are freed of all this frightful machinery of philosophy. We can be men without being scholars; freed from the necessity of consuming our life in the study of ethics, we have at less effort a more sure guide in this immense labyrinth of human opinions. But it is not enough that this guide exists; we must be able to recognize and to follow it. If it speaks to all hearts, why then are there so few who heed it? Well, the fact is that it speaks to us the language of nature, which everything has conspired to make us forget. Conscience is timid and fearful; it loves solitude and peace. The world and its hubbub frighten it. The prejudices to which people attribute it are its most cruel enemies; it flees or is silent in their presence; their loud voice stifles its voice, and prevents it from making itself heard; fanaticism dares to counterfeit it, and to dictate crime in its name. It gives up at length, after being dismissed over and over again; it no longer speaks to us, it no longer answers us; and, after disdaining it so long, it is as difficult to call it back as it was at first to banish it.

How many times in my pursuit of truth I have grown weary of the coldness that I felt within me! How many times sadness and boredom, pouring their poison over my first meditations, made meditations unbearable for me! My arid heart felt for the love of truth only a languishing and lukewarm zeal. I would say to myself: Why torment myself seeking what is not? Moral good is only an illusion; there is nothing good except the pleasures of the senses. Oh, when one has lost the taste for the pleasures of the soul, how difficult it is to regain it! How much more difficult it is to acquire it when one has never had it! If there existed a man wretched enough to have done

44

in all his life nothing which in memory made him pleased with himself and glad to have lived, that man would be incapable of ever knowing himself; and, failing to feel that goodness suits his nature, he would necessarily remain wicked, and would be eternally unhappy. But do you think that there is on the whole earth even one man so depraved that he never surrendered his heart to the temptation to do good? That temptation is so natural and so pleasing that it is impossible to resist it on all occasions; and the memory of the pleasure which it once produced suffices to recall it endlessly. Unfortunately, it is at first difficult to satisfy. Each has a thousand reasons to resist the inclination of his heart. False prudence imprisons him within the limits of the human self; it takes a thousand courageous efforts to dare to go beyond them. To find pleasure in doing good is the reward for doing good, and this reward is obtained only after deserving it. Nothing is more pleasant than virtue; but one must experience it in order to know how pleasant it is. When one seeks to grasp it, like Proteus of the fable, it assumes first a thousand frightful forms, and shows itself finally in its own form only to those who have not let go.

Distinction between the good and the wicked man
Torn unceasingly by my natural feelings which spoke for the common interest, and by my reason which judged everything by selfish interest, I should have wavered all my life in that continual contradiction, doing evil, loving good, and always divided within myself, unless new light had illumined my heart; unless the truth, which finally determined my opinions, had also assured my conduct, and had put me in agreement with myself. It is useless to seek to establish virtue by reason alone; what solid basis can one give to it? Virtue, they say, is the love of order. But can that love prevail in me over the love of my well-being, and ought it to do so? Let them give me a clear and sufficient reason to prefer it. Essentially, their so-called

45

principle is a mere playing with words; for I declare also that vice is love of order, taken in a different sense. There is some moral order wherever there are feeling and intelligence. The difference is that the good man orders his life to serve the whole, and the wicked man makes use of the whole to serve himself. The wicked man makes himself the center of everything; the good man knows his distance from the center and keeps his place at that radius. Thus his life is ordered in relationship to the common center, which is God, and to all the concentric circles, which are God's creatures. If the Divinity does not exist, only the wicked man is reasonable; the good man is but a fool.

Wisdom is the acceptance of the order God has established
O my child! may you be able to feel one day of what a burden one is relieved when, after exhausting the vanity of human opinions and tasting the bitterness of passions, one finds at length so near at hand the way of wisdom, the reward of the labors of this life, and the source of the happiness of which one has despaired! All the duties of the natural law, almost effaced from my heart by the injustice of men, are inscribed there again in the name of eternal justice, which imposes them upon me and which sees me fulfill them. I now feel myself only as the work and the instrument of the great Being who wills good, who does good, and who will bring about my good by the collaboration of my will with his and by the right use of my liberty. I accept the order he establishes, sure of enjoying that order one day myself, and of finding my happiness in it; for what sweeter happiness is there than to feel oneself in harmony with a system where everything is good? Seized by pain, I bear it patiently, aided by the thought that it is transitory, and that it comes from a body which is not mine. If I do a good action without a witness, I know that it is seen, and I record for the other life my conduct in this one. When I suffer an injustice, I

say to myself: The just Being who governs all things will indeed be able to compensate me. The needs of my body, the woes of my life, make the idea of death more endurable for me. Consequently there will be so many fewer bonds to break when I shall have to leave everything.

Why is my soul subject to my senses, and chained to the body which enslaves and hampers it? Of that I know nothing—have I entered into God's decrees? But I can, without rashness, form modest conjectures. I say to myself: If man's spirit had remained free and pure, what merit would he have in loving and following the order which he would find established, and which he would have no interest in disturbing? He would be happy, it is true; but his happiness would lack the most sublime degree, the glory of virtue and his own esteem; he would be only like the angels, and doubtless the virtuous man will be more than they. United with a mortal body by bonds no less powerful than they are incomprehensible, the need of preserving that body excites the soul to consider everything in relation to the body, and to give to it an interest contrary to the general order, which it is however capable of seeing and loving. It is then that the proper use of its liberty becomes at the same time the soul's merit and its reward, and that it prepares for itself an unalterable happiness by combatting its earthly passions and by maintaining itself in its original will.

The wicked are victims of their own evil will If, indeed, in this miserable state in which we live in this life all our original inclinations are legitimate, if all our vices come from ourselves, why do we complain of being subjugated to them? Why do we reproach the author of things for the ills which we make for ourselves, and for the enemies which we arm against ourselves? Ah! let us not spoil man; he will always be good without difficulty, and always happy without remorse. The guilty who declare themselves

driven to crime are as much liars as they are wicked—
how can they help seeing that the weakness they complain
about is their own work; that their first depravation comes
from their will; that by wishing to yield to their temptations, they yield to them finally in spite of themselves, and
make them irresistible? Doubtless it is no longer in their
power not to be wicked and weak, but it was in their power
not to become so. Oh! how easily we should remain mas-
ters of ourselves and of our passions, even during this
life, if, when our habits are not yet acquired, when our
mind begins to develop, we could direct it toward the
objects which it must know in order to appreciate those
which it does not know; if we were willing sincerely to
enlighten ourselves, not to show our brilliance before the
eyes of others, but to be good and wise according to our
nature, to make ourselves happy by practicing our duties!
This study seems to us boring and difficult, because we
think of it only when already corrupted by vice, already
given over to our passions. We fix our judgments and our
esteem before knowing good and evil; and then, gauging
everything by this false standard, we assign to nothing its
proper value.

Happiness achieved by lofty meditations; worship and adoration

There is an age when the
heart, still free but ar-
dent, anxious, avid for the
happiness it does not
know, seeks it with a curious incertitude, and, deceived
by the senses, finally concentrates on a false image of
happiness, and thinks it finds it where it is not. These illusions endured too long in my case. Alas! I knew them
too late for what they were, and I couldn't completely
destroy them: they will last as long as this mortal body
which produces them. At least they tempt me in vain,
for they no longer deceive me. I know them for what they
are, and when I follow them I despise them. Far from
seeing in them the object of my happiness, I see in them
an obstacle to it. I aspire to the moment when, freed

48

from the shackles of the body, I shall be myself without contradiction, without division, and shall need only myself to be happy; in the meantime, I am already happy in this life, because I count for little all its ills, because I consider it almost foreign to my being, and because all the true good which I can draw from it is within my own power.

To raise myself in advance as much as possible to that state of happiness, strength and liberty, I practice sublime contemplations. I meditate upon the order of the universe, not to explain it by vain systems, but to admire it unceasingly, to worship the wise creator who reveals himself through it. I converse with him, I let his divine essence permeate all my faculties; I am moved by his bounty, I bless him for his gifts, but I do not pray to him. What should I ask of him? that he should change for me the course of things, that he should bring miracles to pass in my behalf? I must love above all the order established by his wisdom and maintained by his providence; should I then wish that order to be upset for me? No, that rash wish would merit being punished rather than granted. Neither do I ask of him the power to do good: why ask of him what he has given me? Did he not bestow on me conscience so that I might love the good, reason so that I might know it, liberty so that I might choose it? If I do evil, I have no excuse; I do it because I wish it. To ask him to change my will, is to ask of him what he asks of me; it is to wish him to do my work, and to let me garner the rewards of it. Not to be satisfied with my state is to wish no longer to be a man, it is to wish something other than what is, it is to wish disorder and evil. Source of justice and truth, clement and kind God! In my confidence in thee, the supreme wish of my heart is that thy will be done. By uniting my will with thine, I do what thou dost, I accept thy goodness; I believe that thus I share in advance the supreme happiness which is the reward of it.

In my deserved distrust of myself, the only thing I

ask of him, or rather that I expect of his justice, is to correct my error if I go astray and if that error is dangerous for me. Although I am sincere, I do not believe myself infallible. My opinions which seem to me the truest are perhaps but so many falsehoods, for what man does not cling to his own opinions? And how many men are in agreement on all things? It matters not that the illusion which deceives me comes to me from myself, it is God alone who can cure me of it. I have done what I could to attain the truth; but its source is too lofty—when I lack strength to go farther, of what can I be guilty? Truth must come to me.